EXPLORERS

John
Cabot

Kristin Petrie

ABDO
Publishing Company

visit us at
www.abdopub.com

Published by ABDO Publishing Company, 4940 Viking Drive, Edina, Minnesota 55435. Copyright © 2004 by Abdo Consulting Group, Inc. International copyrights reserved in all countries. No part of this book may be reproduced in any form without written permission from the publisher.

Printed in the United States.

Cover Photos: Corbis, North Wind
Interior Photos: Corbis pp. 4, 5, 7, 10, 12, 13, 15, 17, 19, 23, 26, 27, 28, 29; North Wind pp. 9, 11, 25

Series Coordinator: Stephanie Hedlund
Editors: Kate A. Conley, Kristin Van Cleaf
Art Direction & Cover Design: Neil Klinepier
Interior Design & Maps: Dave Bullen

Library of Congress Cataloging-in-Publication Data

Petrie, Kristin, 1970-
    John Cabot / Kristin Petrie.
        p. cm. -- (Explorers)
    Summary: A biography of the Italian explorer who made several voyages of discovery for England including the discovery of the North American mainland in 1497.
    Includes bibliographical references (p.) and index.
    ISBN 1-59197-593-X
    1. Cabot, John, d. 1498?--Juvenile literature. 2. America--Discovery and exploration--English--Juvenile literature. 3. North America--Discovery and exploration--English--Juvenile literature. 4. Explorers--North America--Biography--Juvenile literature. 5. Explorers--Great Britain--Biography--Juvenile literature. 6. Explorers--Italy--Biography--Juvenile literature. [1. Cabot, John, d. 1498? 2. Explorers. 3. America--Discovery and exploration--English.] I. Title.

E129.C1P48 2004
970.01'7'092--dc22
    [B]
                                                                    2003062920

Contents

John Cabot 4

John's Childhood 6

Before Exploring 8

A Shorter Route 10

Planning 12

Failed Attempt 16

Land Ho! 18

The Great Admiral 22

Third Voyage 26

Lost at Sea 28

Glossary 30

Saying It 31

Web Sites 31

Index 32

John Cabot

Vikings from Scandinavia were some of the first people to explore the northern seas of the Atlantic Ocean. By the 1000s, they had already settled on Iceland and Greenland.

On one journey, Leif Eriksson and his crew landed on a new coast, which they called Vinland. Many scientists now believe this crew was the first to land on Newfoundland, Canada.

No other European braved the trip across the northern Atlantic Ocean until John Cabot. This Italian was working for England when he made his first voyage to North America. Before him, only the Vikings had braved the **uncharted** seas of the north.

Imagine getting in a boat on the largest lake you know. Make sure you can't see land.

John Cabot

1451
Christopher Columbus born

1485
Hernán Cortés born

1450
John Cabot born

1460
Vasco da Gama born

1491
Jacques Cartier bor

Now, go. Good Luck! Hope you find your way. This was all John Cabot had to go on when he decided to explore. Keep reading to find out more about this courageous man.

Leif Eriksson and the Vikings may have been the first explorers to discover North America.

1492
Columbus's first voyage west for Spain

1496
Cabot's first voyage for England

1493
Columbus's second voyage, attempted to colonize Hispaniola

John's Childhood

Giovanni Caboto was born in Genoa, Italy, in 1450. Today, we know him as John Cabot. Little is known about his childhood. But, we do know that John's family moved to Venice, Italy, in 1461.

Venice is a city filled with waterways, the way most cities are filled with streets. To this day, people get around Venice in boats. It is no wonder that a young boy, surrounded by water, would become an explorer by sea.

John's father, Julio, was a seaman and merchant. He owned a spice shop in Venice. At that time, spices came mostly from Asia. So, they were very valuable.

John liked to help his father at the shop. When they were together, Julio may have talked about far away lands. That was probably when John began to dream about exploring the world.

1497
Cabot's second voyage, discovered the Grand Banks; da Gama was first to sail around Africa to India

1496 or 1497
Hernando de Soto born

1498
Cabot's third voyage, may have died; Columbus's third voyage

Would You?

Would you rather be a merchant like Julio, or an explorer like John? Why would you choose that career?

In Venice, Italy, people often use waterways as streets.

1502
Columbus's fourth voyage; da Gama's second voyage

1506
Columbus died

1504
Cortés sailed to the West Indies

Before Exploring

John's formal education is not known. However, the Cabots were fortunate to have lived in wealthy cities with good schools. So, John and other youngsters from Genoa and Venice were able to attend classes. They studied subjects such as reading, writing, and art.

After school, John was expected to be an **apprentice** in the spice shop. It was obvious, however, that he had other things on his mind.

One of the things John Cabot was interested in was sailing. From an early age, he studied mapmaking. He read the book *The Travels of Marco Polo*. And, he continued dreaming of sailing the open seas.

John soon became a merchant, like his father. However, he added the excitement of sailing to his work. He sailed the Mediterranean Sea between Italy and Egypt. On these trips, he traded Italian goods for Eastern spices.

1511
Cortés helped take over Cuba

1510
Francisco Vásquez de Coronado born

1514
De Soto went to the New World

In 1482, John married a woman named Mattea. They had three sons, named Lewis, Sebastian, and Sanctus. In the 1480s, the family moved to Bristol, England.

John Cabot also spent time in London, England.

A Shorter Route

Shortly after Cabot moved to England, Christopher Columbus made a discovery. In 1492, he sailed west from Spain, crossed the Atlantic Ocean, and reached land. Everyone believed this land was the Indies, or Spice Islands.

John Cabot was a mapmaker. This helped him develop his plan.

But, Cabot didn't think Columbus was right. He believed the world was much larger than Columbus claimed. It didn't seem possible to sail directly from Spain to Asia as Columbus said.

Cabot also believed there was a shorter route than the one Columbus had taken. Cabot's mapmaking knowledge had taught him something important. Because the world is round, the farther north you are on a map the closer the **longitudes** are to each other.

1524
Da Gama's third voyage, died in Cochin, India

1519–1521
Cortés conquered the Aztec Empire and claimed Mexico for Spain

1532
De Soto helped attack the Inca Empire

From his beliefs, Cabot came up with a simple but smart plan. He hoped to get to Asia much faster by sailing a shorter route from a better starting point. Cabot would start his voyage from a northern country, England. Columbus had started from Spain, which is farther south.

This plan would have been brilliant, except for one thing. He didn't know yet that North America was in his way.

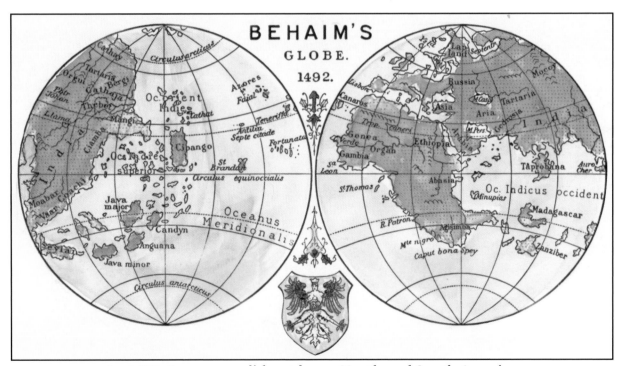

In 1492, Europeans did not know North and South America existed. This map shows their knowledge of the world.

Planning

Living in Bristol, England, fell into Cabot's plan nicely for a couple of reasons. First, he was planning an expedition by sea. Bristol was one of the largest and most important seaports in England. Several expeditions had recently left from there.

Second, England was willing to fund the trip. Cabot had been having trouble getting money to pay for his voyage. Most countries were sending their explorers east to find trading routes to Asia. Cabot wanted to go west.

Unfortunately, it was hard to convince people to give him money to test his plan. King John II of Portugal refused Cabot's request for money. King Ferdinand of Spain did the same. But, Cabot's luck changed in 1496.

King John II of Portugal

1533
De Soto helped take over Cuzco

1534
Cartier's first voyage for France

1535
Cartier's second voyage

1539–1542
De Soto explored La Florida

King Ferdinand of Spain

King Henry VII of England agreed to help Cabot finance his voyage. Businesses in Bristol agreed to help Cabot, too. They hoped to profit from his discoveries.

Europeans believed that China and Japan were rich in gold, **gems**, spices, and silks. Henry VII hoped John Cabot would find a faster route to these riches of Asia. This would make England the greatest trading center in the world.

In addition, Henry VII knew that he could become rich if Cabot's theories were right. Cabot was to give the king one-fifth of any profit he made on his journey. In March 1496, King Henry VII gave Cabot **permission** to sail as a representative of England.

The king wrote a glorious **patent** for the expedition. Henry VII called Cabot his "well-beloved." He wrote that Cabot should seek and discover "whatsoever islands, countries, regions or provinces . . . which before this time were unknown to all Christians."

Would You?

Would you give money to a dreamer like John Cabot? Why or why not?

John Cabot presenting his plan to King Henry VII in 1496

1547 Cortés died	*1557* Cartier died	

1542
Coronado returned to New Spain; de Soto died

1554
Coronado died

1566
Drake's first voyage to the New World

Failed Attempt

In 1496, Cabot made his first attempt at this voyage west. His mission was to find a **Northwest Passage** to Asia. Cabot was the first European explorer to attempt this voyage.

Cabot's attempt may have been the first because sailing so far north was **dangerous**. The cold waters were icy. The wooden ships of that time could not hold up to the ice. And, the waters to the north were unexplored. This, too, was scary.

Cabot set sail from Bristol, England, with one ship. Surprisingly, after reaching nearby Iceland he returned to England. A food shortage and arguments with his crew forced him to return. Dangerous waters and fear of the unknown also helped end this first attempt.

1567
Drake's second voyage

1577
Drake began a worldwide voyage, was first Englishman to sail the Pacific Ocean

1570 and 1572
Drake terrorized the Spanish in the New World

Would you brave the uncharted, icy waters of the north? Why do you think John Cabot turned back on his first voyage?

**Giant icebergs such as this one hindered explorers'
attempts to find the Northwest Passage.**

Land Ho!

On May 20, 1497, Cabot sailed out of the Bristol seaport again. He had a crew of just 18 sailors. Their ship was named the *Matthew*.

The *Matthew* was small for this type of voyage. It was about 70 feet (21 m) long and 18 feet (5 m) wide. It was only about 10 feet (3 m) deep, so it would be able to navigate shallow water. However, the *Matthew* could only carry about 50 tons (45 t) of cargo.

Cabot's first stop may have been in Dursey Head, Ireland. From there, the crew set out for Asia. At least, that's what they thought they were doing. On June 24, 1497, they sighted land. Cabot believed they had reached Asia. The crew went ashore, and Cabot claimed the land for England.

Exactly where Cabot and his crew landed is unknown. Historians guess that it was any of the areas now known as Nova Scotia, Labrador, Cape Breton Island, or Newfoundland.

1588
Drake helped England win the Battle of Gravelines against Spain's Invincible Armada

1581
Drake knighted by Queen Elizabeth I

1596
Drake died

Still others believe he landed farther south, in what is now Maine. But, many believe he landed at Cape Bonavista, Newfoundland.

This replica of the *Matthew* was built in 1997. It sailed to Newfoundland on the anniversary of Cabot's completed voyage.

1728
ames Cook born

1765
Boone journeyed to Florida

1768
Cook sailed for Tahiti

1734
Daniel Boone born

1767
Boone explored Kentucky

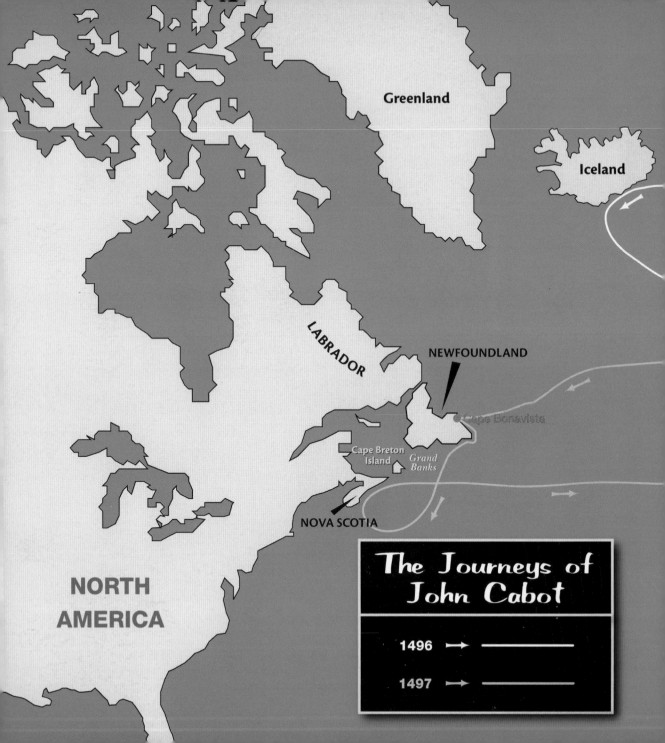

Greenland

Iceland

LABRADOR

NEWFOUNDLAND

Cape Bonavista

Cape Breton
Island

*Grand
Banks*

NOVA SCOTIA

NORTH
AMERICA

The Journeys of John Cabot

| 1496 | ➡ | ———— |
| 1497 | ➡ | ———— |

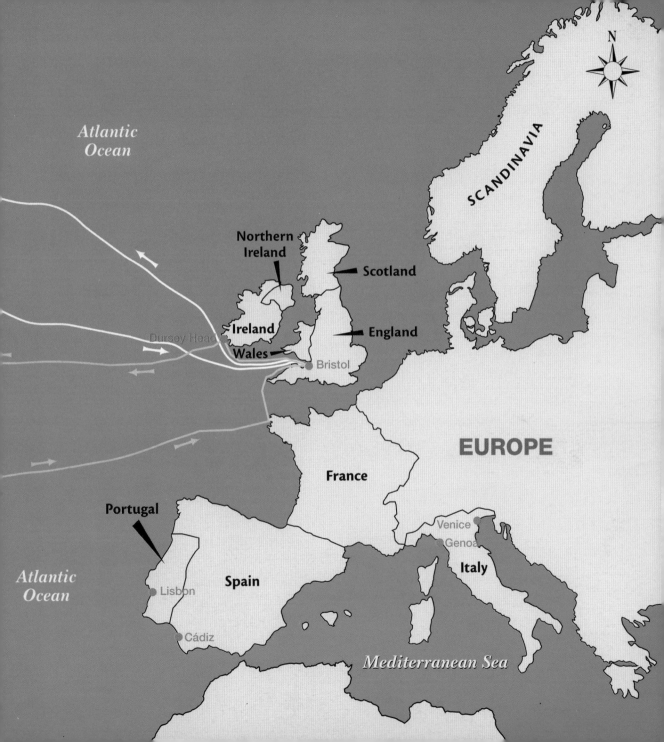

The Great Admiral

Like Christopher Columbus, Cabot thought he had reached Asia. These men simply didn't know that North and South America existed.

Cabot decided to survey the coastline. He may have explored all the way down to Maine. Some people believe Cabot named many of the east coast's islands and capes.

Cabot did not find the jewels, spices, and other riches he was searching for. However, he did find an incredible fishing area. Thousands of cod could be caught just by lowering nets or weighted baskets into the waters. This area is now called Grand Banks.

Opposite page: John Cabot lands at Cape Bonavista, Newfoundland.

1772
Cook's second attempt to discover a seventh continent, became first man to cross the Antarctic Circ

1769
Cook's first attempt to discover a seventh continent; Boone discovered the Cumberland Gap

1778
Cook became the first European to record Hawaiian Islands; Boone captured by Shawnee

1775
Boone cut the Wilderness Road from Virginia to Kentucky

1779
Cook died

After about a month of exploring, the crew headed home. On the return voyage, they took a more southerly route. They landed on the northern coast of France, rather than in England. Finally in August 1497, the *Matthew* and its crew made it back to Bristol, England.

Even though he hadn't found any Eastern cities, Cabot announced that he had reached Asia. So, people thought he had discovered an island off the coast of China!

Cabot was named "The Great Admiral," and the king rewarded him with the sum of ten pounds. Today, it would equal about $10,500. Cabot was also given a **pension** of £20 per year for his discovery. This is about $21,000 per year today.

Opposite page: **John Cabot met natives when he landed on Newfoundland. Yet, he still claimed the land for England.**

1813
John C. Frémont born

1842
Frémont's first independent surveying mission

1820
Boone died

Would you have believed John Cabot when he said he reached Asia? What evidence would you have asked for to confirm his story?

Third Voyage

The king and merchants of England were pleased with Cabot. A **patent** was written for his next voyage. This time, he did not have to beg for money. The king and several merchants offered to pay for the expedition. Cabot had resources for five ships and their crews.

In 1498, Cabot left Bristol with his crew of 300 men. They had enough supplies to last one year. This time, he was to voyage west or south from where he had landed on the first voyage. The aim was to find Japan.

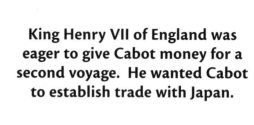

King Henry VII of England was eager to give Cabot money for a second voyage. He wanted Cabot to establish trade with Japan.

1856
Frémont ran for president of the United States but lost

1845-1846
Frémont explored the Great Basin and the Pacific Coast, fought in the Mexican War

1890
Frémont died

Would You?

Would you know what to bring for 300 people for one year? What kinds of supplies would you include if you took a journey like Cabot's?

John Cabot departs from Bristol, England.

1910
acques Cousteau born

1951
Cousteau's first expedition in the Red Sea

1942
Cousteau and Gagnan developed the Aqua-Lung for diving

Lost at Sea

Storms and the rough sea forced one ship back to a port in England or Ireland. Unfortunately, no one knows what happened to the other four ships, or to John Cabot.

This memorial to Cabot can be found on Prince Edward Island, Canada.

JOHN CABOT

THIS PLAQUE HONOURS THE INTREPID SEA
CAPTAIN JOHN CABOT, THE DISCOVERER OF
NORTH AMERICA IN THE YEAR 1497 A.D.,
FOR WHOM CABOT BEACH PROVINCIAL PARK
IS NAMED.

COMMISSIONED BY THE CABOT BEACH PROVINCIAL PARK
"THIS IS YOUR PARK" COMMITTEE

1997
Cousteau died

1974
Cousteau formed the Cousteau Society to protect marine life

Some people think Cabot made it to North America. They believe he explored part of the eastern coast of what is now the United States. Others believe he was lost at sea. Yet others believe he returned to England after his voyage and died there in 1499.

John Cabot may never have found what he was looking for. However, his explorations opened the way for England's colonization of North America. In time, the world would learn the importance of the landmasses that were in the way.

A statue of Cabot at Cape Bonavista

Glossary

apprentice - a person who learns a trade or craft from a skilled worker.

dangerous - able or likely to cause injury or harm.

gem - a precious or semiprecious stone that is cut and polished. Gems are often used in jewelry or as decorations.

longitude - a measure of distance east or west on the earth's surface. This distance is shown on a map as lines that run from the North Pole to the South Pole.

Northwest Passage - a passage by sea between the Pacific and the Atlantic oceans along the northern coast of North America.

patent - an official document giving a person the right or privilege to perform an act or duty.

pension - money for people to live on after they retire.

permission - formal consent.

uncharted - something that is unknown and therefore has not been recorded on a map, chart, or plan.

Cape Breton Island - KAYP BREHT-uhn EYE-luhnd
Giovanni Caboto - joh-VAHN-nee kah-BOH-toh
Labrador - LA-bruh-dawr
Mediterranean Sea - meh-duh-tuh-RAY-nee-uhn SEE
Nova Scotia - NOH-vuh SKO-shuh

To learn more about John Cabot, visit ABDO Publishing
Company on the World Wide Web at **www.abdopub.com**.
Web sites about John Cabot are featured on our Book Links
page. These links are routinely monitored and updated to
provide the most current information available.

Index

A

Asia 6, 10, 11, 12, 14, 16, 18, 22, 24
Atlantic Ocean 4, 10

B

Bristol, England 9, 12, 14, 16, 18, 24, 26

C

Cape Bonavista, Newfoundland 19
Cape Breton Island 18
China 14, 24
Columbus, Christopher 10, 11, 22

D

Dursey Head, Ireland 18

E

education 8
Egypt 8
England 4, 11, 12, 14, 16, 18, 24, 26, 28, 29
Europeans 4, 14, 22

F

family 6, 8, 9
Ferdinand (king of Spain) 12
France 24

G

Genoa, Italy 6, 8
Grand Banks 22
Greenland 4

H

Henry VII (king of England) 14, 24, 26

I

Iceland 4, 16
Indies 10
Ireland 28

J

Japan 14, 26
John II (king of Portugal) 12

L

Labrador 18
Leif Eriksson 4

M

Maine 19, 22
Matthew 18, 24

Mediterranean Sea 8

N

Newfoundland 4, 18
North America 4, 11, 22, 29
Northwest Passage 16
Nova Scotia 18

P

Portugal 12

S

Scandinavia 4
South America 22
Spain 10, 11, 12

T

Travels of Marco Polo, The 8

U

United States 29

V

Venice, Italy 6, 8
Vikings 4
Vinland 4